The Race War
in North Carolina
(1899)

Henry Litchfield West
(1859–1940)

Originally published,
1899

THE RACE WAR IN NORTH CAROLINA

FROM the cold and judicial standpoint of the North, where local environments offer no parallel, the recent tragic revolution in North Carolina was wanton, murderous, and cruel; while, from the Southern point of view, it was not only justifiable, but praiseworthy. Somewhere between these extremes there must be a neutral plane from which the bloody episode can be impartially and dispassionately discussed, with mingled justification and criticism: there must be some unprejudiced, yet observant, chronicler, whose word will be accepted—not as the final one, perhaps, but still as a more or less accurate and important contribution to the working out of a serious problem. In such spirit, at least, I offer this article. Born in the North, of Northern parents, yet residing long enough on the edge of the South to appreciate Southern conditions and not to judge too hastily the Southern people; trained by long years of journalistic experience to observe and to write with careful judgment; and enjoying in the cosmopolitan atmosphere of the national capital a fortunate freedom from the native, unmitigated prejudices of all sections, it is possible that I may be able justly to depict a situation which has attracted the attention of the entire country and which demands the most thoughtful consideration.

When I first entered North Carolina, having been directed to institute an impartial investigation, I had a most imperfect and general understanding of the existing conditions. To be entirely frank, my first glance at the fiery and excited writings of the newspaper editors, together with the passionate exclamations in a series of resolutions adopted at a mass meeting of white men in Goldsboro, held within a short time after my arrival, led me to regard the movement for white supremacy as hysterical. I interviewed Gov. Russell, the first Republican governor elected in North Carolina during a quarter of a century; and he assured me that the reign of terror which existed had its origin in political malice. Consequently, if my mind had any bent, when I finally reached

2

Wilmington in the latter part of October, it was one of opposition to the methods which seemed to have been adopted to suppress the Negro vote; and I was disposed to deprecate the inflammatory state of public feeling. In Wilmington I found a very remarkable condition of affairs. The city might have been preparing for a siege instead of an election. A new rapid-fire gun had been placed in the local armory; nearly two thousand Winchester rifles had been purchased by private citizens; and scarcely a man in the entire city retired at night without a weapon of some kind—rifle, shot-gun, or revolver—by his bedside. The city was officered as if threatened by a foe. Each ward had been divided into blocks; the former in command of a captain, the latter under lieutenants, with a general over all. The lieutenants met their captains almost nightly; and at one of these meetings I had an opportunity to observe that they were earnest, dignified, sober men, heads of families, and owners of property, engaged in the best mercantile and professional pursuits. All shades of political belief were represented. Some of the citizens had voted for Mr. McKinley, and others for Mr. Bryan; some were Gold and some were Silver Democrats; some favored Protection, and others advocated Free Trade: but in the presence of what they believed to be an overwhelming crisis, they brushed aside the great principles that divide parties and individuals, and stood together as one man. Their language indicated the intensity of the situation, as they viewed it. Each lieutenant, when called upon for a report, announced the number of able-bodied men in his block willing to bear arms; while the aggregate number of rifles, shot-guns, and revolvers was also made known. The numbers of women, children, and sick men requiring protection were also given; and the data thus presented were carefully noted down. When I emphasize the fact, that every block in every ward was thus organized, and that the precautionary meetings were attended by ministers, lawyers, doctors, merchants, railroad officials, cotton exporters, and, indeed, by the reputable, taxpaying, substantial men of the city, the extent and significance of this armed movement can, perhaps, be realized. It was not the wild and freakish organization of irresponsible men, but the deliberate action of determined citizens. This condition of affairs naturally excited curiosity, and demanded careful inquiry as to its cause. One could not help wondering why armed men should thus meet nightly in their pleasant and peaceful homes in an American city. Military preparations, so extensive as to suggest assault from some foreign foe, must have had unusual inspiration and definite purpose. Seeking information, I consulted with a number of citizens whose names had been furnished by the Governor himself, and whose position in the community, as I soon learned, entitled their assertions to the highest consideration. They included bank presidents, cotton exporters, prominent railroad officials, and others of equally substantial position. When I asked an explanation of the situation, the answer was given in four words, "The whites must rule." The fiat had gone forth; and it was expected that the Negroes, when they learned that the right of suffrage was to be denied them, would resist. From their churches and from their lodges had come reports of incendiary speeches, of impassioned appeals to the blacks to use the bullet that had no respect for color, and the kerosene and torch that would play havoc with the white man's cotton in bale and warehouse. It was this fear of the Negro uprising in defence of his electorate—of a forcible and revengeful retaliation—that offered an ostensible ground for the general display of arms; but if the truth be told, the reason thus offered was little more than a fortunate excuse. The whites had determined to regain their supremacy; and the wholesale armament was intended to convey to the blacks an earnest of this decision. There would have been rapid-fire guns and Winchester rifles if every church had held a silent pulpit, and every lodge-room where the Negroes met had been empty. White supremacy, therefore, was the magnet that attracted, the tie that bound, the one overwhelming force that dominated everything. To fully appreciate this issue a backward glance is necessary. Wilmington is one of the oldest towns in the United States. Located in the heart of a fertile region, it has prospered. The Cape Fear River affords an easy outlet to the sea. From its wharves cotton is loaded into steamers, each carrying ten to fifteen thousand bales; while the proximity of pine-forests has long made it a famous port for shipping turpentine and rosin. Its broad streets are lined with excellent business structures; and it has all the conveniences and improvements of a modern city. Its social life is proverbially excellent. With all these material advantages, it has the misfortune—and it is a misfortune—to possess a population of which a large majority are Negroes. Of the 25,000 people in the city three-fifths are blacks. While thus numerically strong, the Negro is not a factor in the development of the city or section. With thirty years of freedom behind him and with an absolute equality of educational advantages with the whites, there is not to-day in Wilmington a single Negro savings bank or any other distinctively Negro educational or charitable institution; while the race has not produced a physician or lawyer of note. In other words, the Negro in Wilmington has progressed in very slight degree from the time when he was a slave. His condition can be summed up in a line.

Of the taxes in the city of Wilmington and the county of New Hanover the whites pay 96 per cent; while the Negroes pay the remainder—3 per cent. The Negro in North Carolina, as these figures show, is thriftless, improvident, does not accumulate money, and is not accounted a desirable citizen.

Notwithstanding this, at the ballot-box all men are supposed to be equal; and so the Negroes, if they voted, would rule by mere power of numbers. Until a few years ago their preponderance in local government was neutralized by gerrymandering the bulk of the Negro population into two wards; while to a Democratic legislature was entrusted the task of selecting local magistrates. By these methods a white Board of Aldermen was always secured; and the magistrates were reputable and competent men. Four years ago, however, the white men of the State divided. The Populists, who had many grievances, combined with the Republicans and the 110,000 Negro voters to overthrow the Democratic administration and thus to secure desired reforms. Their efforts were successful, placing the Democrats in a minority. Two years ago the combination won by a majority of 40,000, and, feeling secure against overthrow, began to enact the laws which are primarily responsible for the race war in North Carolina. One of these statutes practically deprived the white citizens of Wilmington of their suffrage by authorizing the Republican governor to appoint five of the ten members composing the Board of Aldermen; the other five to be elected by the five wards, in two of which there were overwhelming Negro majorities. In addition to this, the appointment of magistrates was taken from the legislature, and they were elected by popular vote.

The result of all this can be easily imagined. There were soon thirty-six Negro magistrates, each with power to fine and imprison for all misdemeanors not requiring the cognizance of a jury; there were forty Negro policemen, appointed by the mayor and chief of police chosen by the Negro aldermen; a Negro register of deeds, Negro deputy sheriffs and other Negro subordinate officials in large numbers. My informants asserted that, as a general rule, these Negro officers were ignorant, incapable, and a travesty upon good administration. One of the magistrates, for instance, was a stevedore, elected by the votes of his fellows, and who, when the British vice-consul at Wilmington defended some British sailors before him, announced contemptuously that "De King of England ain't got nothin' to do wid dis co't."

The illiterate deputy sheriffs, unable to write or even read the names upon the warrants given them for execution, were hoodwinked on every corner by persons subject to arrest. The Chief of Police, with his Negro staff, allowed the residents to be assaulted and robbed. Burglaries were of nightly occurrence during the summer months, while the wealthier citizens were at the seashore; and when the householders occasionally caught the midnight thieves, the latter were acquitted by the sympathetic Negro magistrates. In the meantime, the Negroes, who had proved docile and peaceable when under control, appreciated their newly acquired power, and grew insolent and bold. Women were assaulted on the streets; and a Negro editor published an editorial, defaming the virtue of the poor white women of the South. This fanned the flame of Anglo-Saxon resentment to white heat. The evils of maladministration were bad enough: property was not safe; and foreign capitalists, who came to invest, left with their money in their pockets. But this material side of the situation, while it disturbed and paralyzed business interests, did not sting the white blood so savagely as the outspoken contempt of the Negro editor for the white woman's purity.

Ordinarily, social revolutions in the United States are accomplished through the medium of a change in political parties. In Wilmington politics played a most subordinate part. The first definite movement toward the overthrow of Negro rule was taken by the Chamber of

Commerce, a non-partisan organization, which adopted resolutions declaring that the situation was a menace to peace and order, and calling upon "every good citizen to exert his utmost influence and personal effort to effect results which will restore order, protect property, and give security to our lives and homes. The president of the Chamber of Commerce—a New Englander and a Republican—promptly signed this declaration; and every firm connected with tue organization attached its signature with equal alacrity. With this substantial inauguration the movement for white supremacy progressed rapidly. Party divisions disappeared; and the color-line was the plain, recognized, and openly acknowledged issue. Even the Republican postmaster of Wilmington, a Northern man who had never voted the Democratic ticket in his life, recognized this fact. "I had thought at first," he wrote to United States Senator Pritchard," that it was the usual political cry and a fight for office; but I am now convinced that the feeling is much deeper than this, as it pervades the whole community, and there seems to be a settled determination on the part of the property owners, business men, and taxpayers to administer the city and county government."

To illustrate how far removed politics was from the situation, let me say that when it became necessary, in the hope of securing a peaceful settlement, for the regular Democratic candidates for the legislature to withdraw and be succeeded by two gentlemen named by the business men, they acquiesced without delay or protest. It was through this compromise, suggested by the Governor, that the white Republicans and the Negroes failed to nominate a local ticket. When this had been arranged and all incentive for the Negro to vote had been removed, it was hoped and believed that the revolution would be achieved without bloodshed. There was still, however, no disguising of the white men's intentions. They believed that if they paid, as they did, 97 per cent of the taxes, and if they alone had demonstrated their capacity for developing and governing the city, they alone should rule; and this point they were prepared to establish at any cost.

The truce thus declared lasted throughout Election Day. The polls opened and closed without disturbance. By nightfall it was known that the, white men had swept the State; electing a legislature certain, in due time, to repeal objectionable laws and to provide for a constitutional amendment which would prevent the recurrence of Negro rule. The white citizens of Wilmington, who for nearly two years had endured an intolerable condition of affairs with admirable patience, declined to await the slow progress of reform. Flushed with victory, they hastened to emphasize their return to power. While this undue celerity is open to question, one cannot but admire the candor of their action. They resorted to no secrecy or mask. What they did was done in broad daylight; and the entire proceeding suggested the stateliness of a Greek tragedy.

At eleven o'clock in the forenoon nearly one thousand citizens of Wilmington assembled in mass meeting. Clergymen, physicians, lawyers, merchants, clerks, mechanics, and laboring-men were present. Col. Alfred Moore Waddell—one of whose ancestors defied the British stamp collector in 1766, and participated in the conference which led to the Mecklenburg Declaration of Independence —was selected as chairman. A series of resolutions was adopted, declaring that the Negro domination had forever passed and that, in the future, the white man, and the white man alone, should rule. The citizens went further. They decreed, but still without excitement or revengeful speech, that the Negro editor who had published the defamatory article against white women should immediately depart, that his paper should cease publication, and that his plant should be shipped away. A committee of twenty-five was appointed, with Col. Waddell at its head, to enforce the resolutions; and thirty-two of the more prominent Negroes of the city were summoned to meet the committee. Nearly all came in response to the summons. The scene was dramatic. Seated at one end of the room were the twenty-five white men: at the other end sat the thirty-two Negroes. The whites were anxious, but determined; the Negroes, cowed and terror-stricken. The resolutions were read and, in answer to a query from one of the blacks as to the meaning of a phrase, reread. There was no discussion, no argument. The whites delivered their ultimatum, gave the Negroes until the following morning to make answer, and declared the meeting adjourned. The whites and blacks then passed silently out into the night.

On that night, as on the night before, the streets were guarded by white citizens; but there was no outbreak. In momentary fear of the fire alarm, men slept in their clothes and with their weapons beside them. On the following morning the streets presented the strange spectacle of men ordinarily engaged in the quiet walks of life, proceeding to their places of business with rifles on their shoulders. At eight o'clock they assembled in the public hall, to await the answer of the Negroes. None came. By a strange error, the messenger to whom it had been entrusted placed it in a letter-box-where it remained until the next day—instead of carrying it direct to Col. Waddell's house, as he had been instructed by his Negro brethren. There being no answer, therefore, seventy-five men were called for and five hundred swung into line. The morning papers had prominently published in capital letters the names of the citizens, numbering 457, signing the resolutions of the previous day, so that there was no concealment, no lack of identification. The procession moved out of the hall in column of fours. An eye-witness writes:

"Under thorough discipline and under command of officers, capitalists and laborers marched together: the lawyer and his client were side by side. Men of large business interests kept step with clerks. It was not a mob. It was a gathering of white men who were determined to teach a lesson, a lesson which should be practical, and contain no element of doubt. The work, when the fated building which held the printing-press was reached, was quickly done. Nothing that looked like any part of a printer's establishment was permitted to escape demolition. When this work had been accomplished, the building was found to be on fire. One of the men who was there to destroy the printing-press turned in an alarm. The engines came thundering to the scene, the firemen laid their hose, and commenced the work of salvation. No attempt was made to hinder their work; but no help was rendered. Men looked on with grim faces; possibly exulting, but not boisterous. It was no holiday, no light comedy performance to be carried on amid merriment and laughter; but every man seemed impressed with the responsibility of his self-imposed duty. Other buildings caught fire; but men with guns in their hands climbed upon the roofs and extinguished the igniting shingles. There was no desire to injure property not concerned in the deed for which the punishment was inflicted. The children of a neighboring school became almost hysterical through fear; and their principal was told that they were free to go home or stay, that no harm could or should come to them. An old Negro woman, excited by the scene, stood upon the sidewalk and with all the religious fervor of her race, invoked the wrath of Heaven. She was watched with silent amusement; and as the flames succumbed to the floods of water, the order to return was given and each man went to his home. This was the first chapter of the tragedy. The second was enacted an hour or so later, when some Negroes fired upon a small group of white men at a point fully a mile distant from the printing-office. The fire was returned; three negroes being killed, and three wounded. As one of the uninjured Negroes moved away, he levelled a Winchester, according to the statement of eye-witnesses, at a white man standing upon the threshold of a house, fired, and dangerously wounded him. The Negro ran into a house, but was pursued, dragged out, and riddled with bullets. Desultory firing, with more or less fatal results, followed in various parts of the city; and in the afternoon the local military took possession of the disturbed district.

Additional forces of militia were summoned from surrounding towns. At night the Mayor was forced to resign, and the Chief of Police, who had remained in the city hall during the trouble, was also displaced; white men, selected by the citizens in mass meeting, taking their places. Thousands of Negroes, terrorstricken, fled to the woods and swamps; and white men who had become objectionable, because of their affiliations with the Negroes, were escorted out of the city by armed processions. Events moved rapidly. The new Mayor, Col. Waddell, and the new Board of Aldermen—the former members having resigned—issued a proclamation, commanded order to be restored, interfered to prevent threatened lynching, sent squads of men to protect trembling laborers to their homes, and organized committees to go out into the woods and assure the fleeing Negroes that they could return without harm. New police officers were sworn in. The old administration could secure only fifteen men to serve on Election Day with pay; the new administration swore in three hundred citizens without delay and with

services free. On the next day the request
that all citizens leave their arms at home
and resume their former avocations was
complied with. The bloody drama was
over. It is easy to understand that, while
the events which led up to this tragic
dénoument were in progress in
Wilmington, the situation throughout
North Carolina was almost equally intense.
The conditions which prevailed in
Wilmington existed throughout the entire
eastern section of the State, and were
especially unbearable in the six or seven
counties which comprised the "black belt."
In one of these counties, Craven, in which
the shipping port of Newbern, with 12,000
inhabitants, is situated, the Negroes filled
sixty-six of the local offices; the State
senator was a Negro who had thrice been
convicted of forgery; and the candidate for
county treasurer, the Negro keeper of a
bar-room. In all of the counties where the
Negroes were in a majority, Negroes had
secured positions on the school
committees, although, as I was informed,
notoriously unfitted for such offices. Young
white girls, many of whom taught school as
the only means of raising enough money to

insure them a college education, were compelled to apply to these Negro committeemen for appointment; and their dependent position was emphasized by the necessity of visiting the Negroes monthly in order to have their warrants properly certified. The character of the men selected thus to supervise the educational system can best be illustrated by the statement that, under the law of North Carolina, committeemen, when unable to write their own names, are authorized to affix their marks to warrants and other documents. The repugnance which these white girls experience in thus being compelled to seek favors at the hands of Negro committeemen may not be appreciated by the whites in the North and may seem to be without adequate foundation; but apart from this purely racial sentiment, there is no doubt that in many cases the antipathy was increased by the utter contempt which education feels for ignorance, the inspections and examinations conducted by the Negro committeemen being farcical in the extreme. In addition to this, the irritations of Negro control were illustrated in other directions. From a statement recently made by Senator McLaurin, of South Carolina, some interesting figures are taken. In discussing the character of the Negro municipal office-holders, he says: "Take the city of Greenville, North Carolina, for example, where the taxable property aggregates three-quarters of a million dollars in value. The Board of Aldermen levies the taxes and orders the expenditures. One of the Negro aldermen pays 84 cents in taxes; another, 63 cents; the other two pay nothing. The total taxes paid by the Negro aldermen is $1.47. The mayor, a white man elected by Negro votes, pays 43 cents in taxes; the policeman none, the night watchmen none, the chief of police 25 cents. The revenues of this town amount to $5,500 per annum, of which $2,830 goes to pay the salaries of the non-taxpaying Negro officeholders."

Whether or not this condition justified the white men in refusing to submit to a continuance of Negro rule is a question which will, without doubt, be variously answered in different sections of the United States; but the fact remains that in North Carolina it was decided in the negative. This decision could not be enforced, however, except by disfranchising the Negro, to secure which result two methods only seemed to present themselves; viz., (1) the Negro must either be frightened away from the polls, or else (2) he must be forcibly resisted when he undertook to deposit his ballot. The first method offered the least objection and promised the minimum amount of open disturbance; and in many of the counties in the "black belt," therefore, the picturesque "Red Shirt" brigades were organized for the acknowledged purpose of terrorizing the Negroes. At one of the Red Shirt rallies, which I attended, at Laurinburg, near the South Carolina line, there were a thousand men on horseback, all wearing the lurid and significant garment. For ten miles through pine-forest and cotton plantation these men rode, singling out the Negro hamlets as the especial object of their visitation; while in the afternoon they listened to an impassioned address in which they were advised to win the election—peaceably if they could, forcibly if they must. The orator described the methods which prevailed in his own county of Halifax for neutralizing the Negro rule. "When a Negro constable comes with a warrant for a white man in his hands," said the speaker, "he leaves with a bullet in his brains." This declaration was loudly applauded. The Red Shirters, as they were called, were the picturesque adjuncts of the remarkable campaign; but they were not border ruffians, as someone characterized them. They were farmers, bankers, school teachers, merchants, in fact, the element in a community which stands highest in the social and commercial scale.

While in Wilmington the white supremacy movement had its inspiration and encouragement almost entirely in the desire of the business and taxpaying interests to be rid of the evils of bad government, there is no question that the issue in the central and western portions of the State, where the Negroes did not predominate, was purely political. It must be remembered, of course, that unless the Fusion legislature was voted out of power, the repeal of obnoxious laws was impossible; and to secure the overthrow of such a legislature the coöperation of all the whites in the State was absolutely necessary. Even with this fact, however, the politicians who had no personal concern in the solution of the problem were keen enough to see that white supremacy meant Democratic supremacy; and they labored for both con amore.

The result was that in all sections of North Carolina, from the mountainous border of the west to the sand-dunes on the Atlantic shore, the doctrine of antagonism to the Negro was preached from every stump, and reiterated in the columns of every newspaper. The most rabid and inflammatory editorials appeared; the local poets trimmed their wings to flights of exalted rhetoric, and declared in burning rhyme that "The whites must rule the land or die"; the ordinary news of the day was crowded out to afford room for daily repetitions of the Negro editor's defamatory article and such extracts from Republican speeches as might tend to heat still further the Southern blood. The Negro himself was pilloried as the quintessence of all that was brutal and dangerous. Especial prominence was given to items, the purport of which is evidenced in the following headlines, all of which are taken from a single issue of a Raleigh daily:

"Estimable Lady Grossly Assaulted by a Black Negro!" "An Impertinent Negro Puts in His Lip and Narrowly Escapes Being Roughly Handled!" "Black Scoundrel Assaults a White Man!" "Negro Youths Assault and Rob a Venerable and Highly Esteemed Citizen on a Principal Street!" "Insolent Negroes Parade, Arm Themselves, and March through the Streets of Wilmington!" In addition to this, the most violent communications found ready entrée into the columns of the daily press throughout the State; and whether it was the bloodthirsty correspondent who appealed for an immediate lynching, or "a farmer's wife" who urged the white voter to save her sex from outrage, the effect was the same. From the pulpits the doctrine of white supremacy was preached in the same breath with the story of Christ's love. The oratory from the stump was lava-like. Men accounted in their communities as conservative boldly advocated violent measures. One candidate for State Senator advised a mass meeting of white citizens to "win the election, peaceably if possible, but win it in any way you can." Another orator—a former judge described with evident gusto how five hundred of his fellow-citizens in a county had waited upon a Republican orator and driven him off because of his "slanderous expressions" in advising Negroes to put their arms around white girls; a third declared that the Negro editor in Wilmington ought to be food for catfish in Cape Fear River; and still another countenanced the assassination of the Governor who had brought Negro rule upon the State. Stimulated by such angry flood, the passions of the people grew more intense; and at the end of the campaign nothing except the most fiery utterances satisfied the excited crowds. In

Wilmington, on the night before election, the greatest applause at a public meeting was bestowed upon a citizen who coolly laid his six-barrelled revolver upon the chairman's table and boldly announced his intention of using it in the furtherance of the "white man's cause."

What were the Negroes doing all this time? Some of them were undoubtedly sullen and resentful; but the great mass of them were in a state of terror amounting almost to distress. At the first sign of actual hostility their white leaders deserted them; and in the face of murderous antagonism they would willingly have bartered their right of suffrage for a glimpse of the white flag of peace. An affidavit of a railroad employee attests the fact that the actual outbreak in Wilmington was precipitated by a Negro; but all testimony agrees that there was nothing like a general uprising. On the contrary, as soon as the first shot was fired the Negroes fled by thousands to the woods, where their pitiable condition excited the sympathy of the whites. I quote from a local newspaper:

"The most distressful circumstance in connection with the riot, so far as the Negroes are concerned, resulted from the panic among these people. Women and children and men fled to the woods by thousands on Thursday and Friday. The roads were lined with them, some carrying their bedding on their heads and whatever effects could be carried. It was pitiable to see the children hurrying in fright after their parents. People who come into the city from the country report that these terror-stricken Negroes slept in the woods Thursday and Friday nights. They huddled around without any protection overhead and many had nothing but the ground to sleep upon. Many fled without taking a quilt or blanket, so that most of them had no covering. Although the weather is yet mild, it is sufficiently cool, however, to cause suffering, and this, added to the fact that they had little or nothing to eat, made their condition pitiable. In their hunger and distress, the people in the country assisted them as much as they could. They tried to induce the refugees to come back to the city, but they would not hear of it. The most alarming reports went out to them about the slaughter of Negroes in the city, and in fact, the telegraph carried out the most wildly exaggerated messages. Some of the Negroes are coming back to the city, and report their experience as awful."

Having thus sketched, in broad lines, the inception of the race war in North Carolina, as well as the conflict in which it culminated, it would be interesting, as well as profitable, to consider the verdict which ought to be rendered upon the facts. This, however, is not the purpose of the present article. The academic discussion of the Negro problem opens too wide a field to be entered upon here. Nevertheless, I desire to call attention to the fact, which does not seem to have been anywhere noted, that the political effect of the campaign, from a national point of view, might have been extremely curious. Under the pressure exerted by the white leaders, the Republican and Populist forces were disintegrated in every section of the State, while in the "black belt" the Negroes did not dare to vote; so that an almost solid Democratic delegation was elected from the State to Congress. In the Wilmington district a Republican majority of 5,000 in 1896 gave place to a Democratic majority of 6,000,—a gain for the Democrats of 11,000 votes. No one for a moment supposes that this was the result of a free and untrammelled ballot; and a Democratic victory here, as in other parts of the State, was largely the result of the suppression of the Negro vote. Notwithstanding this, there were several days after the recent election, while the control of the National House of Representatives hung in the balance, when it seemed as if that control might depend upon the seven Democratic Congressmen elected in North Carolina. Had this proved to be the case, the situation would have been most anomalous. We would have seen the House organized by a Democratic majority, for members are seated on prima facie returns,—when its moral right, if not legal authority, was open to serious question. Happily this spectacle has been avoided; but it is a warning to thoughtful people of the serious problems which the future may offer. The situation demands the wisest statesmanship, with certain factors already laid down. No one who has witnessed the condition of affairs in the South can believe that the Negro is, at the present time, capable of governing. All his efforts in this direction have been lamentable, direful failures. On the other hand, no one acquainted with the spirit and temper of the Southern people believes that the Negro, whatever his future capacity may be, will be allowed to govern the white race. These two assertions—that the Negro cannot govern, and that the white man will not let him govern—are axioms. While the Negro continues shiftless, ignorant, superstitious, and incompetent, there is a justification for the refusal to give him absolute control over invested capital, commercial interests, and municipal matters. At the same time, the casting and the counting of his ballot are his constitutional rights; and so long as these are denied him, there is a confession that our vaunted scheme of universal suffrage is a failure and a farce.

They will be denied him, however, even at the muzzle of the rifle; and as long as he threatens to exercise his rights, just so long will the South remain solid.

At this point the question broadens from local interest into national significance; because when the possibility of Negro domination has been removed from the South, that section will express its free thought on national questions. There will then be disintegration in what is now a compact and defensive mass. The South is Democratic because it would escape Negro rule in local offices, and Negroes in collectorships, post-masterships, and other Federal positions; and thus the South votes for the free coinage of silver as it would vote for unlimited greenbacks, Government ownership of railroads, or anything else that the Democratic party might countenance in its platform. Eliminate the all-powerful reason for solidity, and Gold and Silver, Protection and Free Trade, Anti-Expansion and Colonial Acquisition will be the penetrating wedges. How is this much-desired consummation to be attained? Shall the suffrage of the Negro be restricted by educational or property tests, and the South be granted representation in Congress and the Electoral College on the basis of the vote actually cast? Or shall we look to the Negro to work out his own salvation? In the latter event, he has a long and thorny road to tread, in comparison with which the way that Bunyan's pilgrim travelled was a path of roses.